ookie

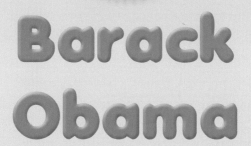

Barack Obama

by Joanne Mattern

Content Consultant

Nanci R. Vargus, Ed.D.
Professor Emeritus, University of Indianapolis

Reading Consultant

Jeanne Clidas, Ph.D.

Children's Press®
An Imprint of Scholastic Inc.
New York Toronto London Auckland Sydney
Mexico City New Delhi Hong Kong

Library of Congress Cataloging-in-Publication Data
Mattern, Joanne, 1963-
  Barack Obama / by Joanne Mattern; poem by Jodie Shepherd.
    p. cm. — (Rookie biographies)
  Includes index.
  ISBN 978-0-531-24735-8 (library binding) ISBN 978-0-531-24701-3 (pbk.)
  Obama, Barack—Juvenile literature. 2. Presidents—United States—Biography—
Juvenile literature. 3. African Americans—Biography—Juvenile literature.
I. Shepherd, Jodie. II. Title.
  E901.1.O23M37 2013
  973.932092—dc23 [B]   2012035025

Produced by Spooky Cheetah Press
Poem by Jodie Shepherd

Printed in the United States of America 141

SCHOLASTIC, CHILDREN'S PRESS, ROOKIE BIOGRAPHIES®, and associated logos
are trademarks and/or registered trademarks of Scholastic Inc.

1 2 3 4 5 6 7 8 9 10 R 22 21 20 19 18 17 16 15 14 13

Photographs © 2013: AP Images: 24 (J. Scott Applewhite), 7 inset, 8, 12 (Obama
Presidential Campaign), 20, 30 left, 31 top (Ron Edmonds); Getty Images: 11 (Laura
S. L. Kong), cover (Mandel Ngan/AFP), 23 (Pete Souza/The White House), 28
(Win McNamee); Media Bakery/Hill Street Studios: 31 center top; Polaris Images:
19, 31 center bottom (Anne Ryan), 15; REX USA: 26; Shutterstock, Inc.: 3 top left
(Lightspring), 3 bottom (Rudy Balasko), 3 top right, 30 right (Vladislav Gurfinkel);
White House Photo/Pete Souza: 4, 16, 31 bottom.

Maps by XNR Productions, Inc.

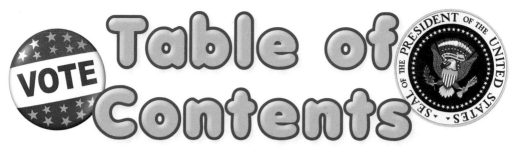

Table of Contents

Meet Barack Obama 5

A New Life 14

Working for Change 18

Mr. President 22

Timeline 28

A Poem About Barack Obama 30

You Can Be a Leader 30

Glossary 31

Index 32

Facts for Now 32

About the Author 32

Meet Barack Obama

Barack Obama (buh-ROK oh-BAH-muh) is the 44th **president** of the United States. He is our country's first African-American President.

President Obama was elected in 2008.

The state of Hawaii is made up of eight islands. In the picture, Barack is playing on a beach in Hawaii with Gramps.

Barack was born in Hawaii on August 4, 1961. He lived with his mother and grandparents. Barack's father did not live with them.

FAST FACT!

Barack called his grandmother "Toot" and his grandfather "Gramps."

Alaska

CANADA

Washington

Oregon

Nevada

California

★ Honolulu

Hawaii

PACIFIC
OCEAN

MEXICO

MAP KEY

▢ Hawaii

★ **City where
Barack Obama
was born**

Barack with his mother, stepfather, and sister, Maya.

Barack's mother married a man from a faraway country called Indonesia. The family moved there when Barack was six years old. When he was 10, Barack's mother sent him back to live with his grandparents in Hawaii. She wanted her son to go to school in America.

The President loves to play basketball. He played on his high school team. His teammates called him "Barry O'Bomber."

Barack graduated from high school in 1979. First he went to college in California. Later he went to college in New York City. Barack studied hard and did well.

FAST FACT!

When he was young, Barack went by the name "Barry."

After college, Barack got a job in Chicago. He worked with people in poor neighborhoods. He helped them make their community better.

This is a picture of Barack in New York City, where he went to college.

A New Life

Barack went to law school in Massachusetts. In the summer, he took a job in Chicago. He fell in love with a young woman named Michelle. In 1992, they got married. After law school, Barack and Michelle lived in Chicago.

Barack and Michelle pose with their moms.

Malia

Sasha

The Obamas' daughters are named Malia and Natasha. Natasha is always called "Sasha."

In 1996, Barack ran for the Illinois Senate and won! As a state **senator**, he helped make the state's laws for eight years. A law is a rule that everyone has to follow.

Barack and Michelle had two daughters while he was a state senator.

Working for Change

Next Barack became a U.S. senator. He was helping to make laws for the whole country. He wanted to help people change their lives for the better.

Senator Obama greets one of his supporters.

In 2004, the United States was getting ready to **elect** a new president. A meeting called a **convention** was held to pick a person to run for the office. Barack gave a great speech. After the convention, people all over the United States knew who he was.

More than nine million people watched Barack's speech on television.

Mr. President

A few years later, Barack decided to run for president. In 2008, he was elected President of the United States. President Obama lives in the White House with his family and their dog, Bo. He also works there.

The President is playing with Bo on the lawn of the White House.

President Obama signs
a law about health care.

President Obama has a very hard job. He is the leader of all the people who live in the United States. He works with other American leaders to make new laws for the country.

Here, the President is meeting with the queen of England.

President Obama also meets with leaders from other countries. He wants the United States to be friendly with other nations.

Barack has visited 40 countries since he became president. He has also visited all 50 U.S. states.

Timeline of Barack Obama's Life

1997
starts first term in Illinois Senate

1961
born on August 4

1985
moves to Chicago

In this photo, President Obama and his family celebrate his victory.

In 2012, Barack ran for president again. He defeated Mitt Romney to win a second term in office.

2004
elected to the
U.S. Senate

2012
re-elected
president

2004
delivers a speech
at the Democratic
National Convention

2008
elected president
of the United States

A Poem About Barack Obama

Barack Obama is our forty-fourth president.
He works hard for every U.S. resident,
and does his best the whole day long
to keep our country free and strong.

You Can Be a Leader

- You can learn to use words to help people understand new ideas.

- Study hard in school and learn as much as you can about important issues.

- Work to make things better for people in your school or your neighborhood.

Glossary

convention (kuhn-VEN-shun): a large meeting of people who have the same interests

elect (i-LEKT): to choose someone by voting

president (PREZ-uh-duhnt): the elected leader of a country

senator (SEN-uh-tor): a member of a group of people who make laws for a state or country

Index

Chicago 13, 14, 17

early life 6, 9, 10, 13

family 14, 17, 22

making laws 17, 18, 25

meeting foreign
  leaders 26

president 5, 10, 21, 22,
  25, 26, 29

re-election 29

senator 17, 18

speech 21

White House 22

Facts for Now

Visit this Scholastic Web site for more information on Barack Obama:
www.factsfornow.scholastic.com
Enter the keywords **Barack Obama**

About the Author

Joanne Mattern has written more than 250 books for children. She especially likes writing biographies because she loves to learn about real people and the things they do. Joanne also enjoys writing about science, nature, and history. She grew up in New York State and still lives there with her husband, her four children, and an assortment of pets.